Facts of Life

Reflections on Ignorance and Intelligence

Facts of Life

Reflections on Ignorance and Intelligence

Rehana Shamsi

First Printing: 2016

ISBN: 978-0-9950082-0-5

Author Photo by Tariq Khan
Cover Image © Kynata/Shutterstock

Follow Rehana Shamsi at www.facebook.com/RShamsi.Poetry

For my gracious parents,
and
for Zia and Shwe Win,
Zafar and Farah,
Anwar, Alina, Zainab and Nabeel

Contents

Acknowledgements xi
Introduction xiii

Awareness after Repression 3
A Brave Little Girl 5
A Spark of Freedom 8
Audacity 10
Bypassing Rules 12
A Mind at Peace 13
Sweet Memories 14
Cold Winds of Helplessness 15
Journey from Confinement to Freedom 16
Evenly Trapped 18
Consignment of New Ambitions 20
Fragile Sanity 21
Golden Dreams 22
Robbers 23
Heavenly Intervention 24
When My Brain is Lost 25
Icy Rock of Grievances 26
Ignorance 28
Intelligence 29
Renewed Tune of Insight 30
Shore of Emancipation 32
Taj Mahal 33
Valiant Façade 34
Virtues and Vices 36
Symphony of Love 38

Gender Disparity 41
The Secret of Tranquility 43
Sacrificial Lamb 44
The Bride 46

Resurrection 49
Sometimes Asleep, Others Awake 51

Grimful Glee or Total Victory 55
At the Mercy of a Craftsman............................. 58
Brutal Encounter 60
Resurrection 61
Restored Gift... 64

Health **67**
Health... 69
Ready to Negotiate... 70
Sweaty Terror... 72
Underwritten Existence..................................... 74

Migration... **75**
Jewel of Freedom.. 77
Moving from New York 82
Argue Not... 84

Family **87**
My Family by My Side....................................... 89
A Window in My Past.. 90
A Spring-like Day in Autumn............................ 92
Our Little Angel 94
The Perfect Creation 95
A Gift from Heaven 96
My Precious Grandchildren 97
Contentment.. 98
Glorious Moments 99
Two Beautiful Flowers 100
Gratitude 101
A Sunflower at its Glorious Height 102
Stilled Forever... 104
Fabric of Support 106

Facts of Life.. **107**
Aloneness... 109
Invest in Beautiful Thoughts.............................. 110

Ailing Emotions 172
Enormous Piece of Cloud 174
Excel and Rely 176
Seasons... 177
On Cloud Nine 178
In Sapphire Blue 179
Words Are Our Friends..................................... 180
Colossal Glory 183
T-Chamber vs. T-Chamber 184
Mathematical Death 186
From Harsh Winter to Pleasant Spring 188
My Shrine.. 190

— ᷣ —

Comfort Zone 111
Capture the Moment... 112
Anger, Bitterness, Criticism 113
The Sweet Fruit of Patience 114
Clear Mind... 115
History Rests in… 116
Anger... 117
Looking Back 118
Facts of Life... 120
Two Faces of Silence 122
Sense of Humor.. 124
Soldier be at Peace 126
Words of Appreciation 128
Marriage 129

Old Age **131**
Before Resting in Soft Peace.. 133
A Dose of Bitter Medicine 134
Rocking in Past Glories.. 135
Short-lived Glory.. 136

Bereavement... **139**
Melancholic Heart and Solicitous Mind............................ 141
A Faint Smile... 144
A Goodbye that was Never Said 147
Infant Joys, Matured Sorrows 150
In Memory of Dr. Emil Orsini... 152

Nine-Eleven **155**
Our Great Nation Stood Tall 157
Soy Milk and Chocolate Cookie 161

Curiosity and others **165**
Life Long Commitment... 167
A Talent... 170
Curiosity 171

Acknowledgements

My deepest gratitude goes to my dear professor Dr. John Snyder of College of Staten Island, The City University of New York. This book of poetry would not have been possible without his encouragement and guidance.

A very special thank you to my son Zafar Shamsi for his unwavering dedication and generosity of time. Zafar, thank you for taking care of every minute detail while formatting, proofreading, and setting layout. Your resolute efforts have paid off.

Thank you very much professors Drs. Margery Cornwell, Timothy Gray, Arnold Kantrowitz, Steven Monte, and Jim Tolan for your guidance, and using your pen on my writings.

I am thankful to all my tutors at College of Staten Island (CUNY) for their constructive instructions. Their advice enabled me to improve my work.

Thank you to my creative writing course classmates. I learned so much each time your works were read in the class.

My sincere thanks to Mary Newberry, my editor extraordinaire, for her exceptional work on my poems. Mary, your vigilant eyes were thorough, and your editorial notes were educational, helpful, and clear. I greatly appreciate your dedication.

I also want to thank my dear friend Robin Newell for tutoring and for directing my attention to different ways of formatting a poem.

I am very appreciative of my family—Zia and Shwe Win, Zafar and Farah, Anwar and Alina, and to my precious grandchildren, Zainab and Nabeel. Their love, care, understanding, and their warm relationship with each other enabled me to do my writing with peace of mind. Thank you my compassionate family for making my life easy and pleasurable.

In eight of the ninety-six poems in this collection, I borrowed lines from the works of other writers and poets. I sincerely apologize for my failure to credit these talented individuals as I cannot recall their names or the publications from which these lines were borrowed. I hope someone will jog my memory so they can be properly acknowledged.

I have tried to put all the borrowed lines in quotation marks. Some of the lines, such as those in *Sense of Humor*, *A Talent*, and *Words are Our Friends*, are probably from non-fiction books. These lines became part of my memory and I have written poems around them or using them.

The lines used in *Rocking in Past Glories*, *The Bride*, *Facts of Life*, *Glorious Moments*, and *Underwritten Existence* I found in my scrapbook.

— ॐ —

Introduction

I was born in India but my family moved to Pakistan soon after the partition in 1947. I grew up in a conservative society where girls were not sent to school. Gender disparity was the rule of society. Before marriage women were under strict control of their fathers or elder brothers and after an arranged marriage, husbands were their absolute masters. Women were not allowed to make any decisions or leave home without their husbands' permission.

Luckily my parents did not believe in gender discrimination. My sister and I enjoyed as much freedom as our two brothers. I was the first girl in my family to go to school.

These poems focus on my relationship with my former society. I voice the nearly ineffable emotional trauma that South Asian women suffer under male sovereignty—the ignominy of extreme suppression.

A significant number of my poems are about social issues I observed while growing up. It still hurts to think of all the injustices I have witnessed. I was fortunate that my family was much more open minded than those of my friends.

As time has passed, girls have started going to school and have become aware of the issues. They have started to speak out against discrimination, unfair treatment, and abusive customs and traditions. A substantial number of educated women are questioning, challenging, and resisting these inequalities.

While there is progress and things are slowly improving for the educated urban women, the rural areas have not seen any change in this regard. Women are still suppressed and girls are still forcibly married off to much older men. Women are denied education and still continue to live subjugated lives.

I have tried to bring these issues to the forefront and have juxtaposed some poems to make it clear that to unshackle ourselves from unfair restraints, women have to try audaciously to achieve their rightful place in society. In my writing, I want women to realize that suppression is not our destiny if we learn to stand up for ourselves. I compare pleasant and unpleasant circumstances to make sense of my past and present.

I hope my poetry will bring more awareness to its readers.

Writing restores buried integrity and individuality.

Awareness after Repression

In South Asia, under male sovereignty, women suffer ineffable emotional trauma. They have to deal with archaic and abusive customs, unfair treatment, and caustic misery of subjugation. Educated women are more aware of it and are trying to unshackle themselves from the ignominy of loss of identity.

A Brave Little Girl

A brave little girl
with a warm little heart, had a smooth start.

Under the umbrella of love and attention,
she learned self-reliance.

Secure and content,
the girl breezed through her youth carrying

     innocence from dew,
     coolness from moon,
     warmth from sun,
     fragrance from flowers,
     freedom from wind.

She ambled into adulthood ready
for life-long commitment
determined to commence perpetual union
with devotion and endurance.

     The stretch of contentment fell short,
     once blissful association turned bristly.

     The girl realized

     weight of diminished attention,
     and denial of her rights,
     broke her heart, disturbed her soul,
     burden of infinite compromises,
     robbed off pleasure from her life.

     Lovely roses (from the union),
     auspiciously held her heart.

By the dusk of her life
she learned to be alive
with thorns and thistles
amid delightful roses,
with thunder and lightning
on her hazy, misty sky,
with bitter cold days and
no warmth to rely on.

    Loss of identity,
    exhausted her spirits,
    incapacitated her mind.

She coveted, constantly,
for treasured possession,
and yearned, continually,
for emancipation.

The girl with dismal heart,
gravely disintegrated,
tried to fly again, but
with wings already gone,
could not make it to the sky.

    A mentor touched her life
    with wisdom and insight,
    he made the girl realize

racking the past was malignant for a wounded heart,
forgiveness was the requisite for extinguishing the fire of anger,
rainbow of hope would conquer the woes of her past.

Detaching from the aching past, was
lifting a rugged mountain from a trodden heart.

To liberate her stretched-out existence,
the girl strove to learn the art of healing.

Moon smiled with its
ever-confident cool,

morning dew invited her
to wash away blues,

glorious sun helped visualize
rainbow on the sky,

fragrant flowers
inebriated her soul,

refreshing winds
assisted her beyond the mist
of nerve-racking thoughts.

— ॐ —

A Spark of Freedom

I was a casualty without being dead,
cold in audacity, enthusiastic in ambitions,
executed by rules of compliance,
no right, whatsoever, of making decisions,
dictated by emissaries of independence.

Witnessing my burial in installments,

> daring no questions,
> offering no denials,
> concealing a spark of freedom,
> trying not to go into seclusion
> like a small wood pigeon,

I looked through the window of my soul,

I Wasn't Bent Beyond Repair.

To unravel tyranny of manipulation,
I searched for deliverance

> under each wrong lies right,
> weakness disguises in strength,
> night embraces morning, and
> darkness departs in the presence of sun.

I struggle to unshackle my existence
from the chain of subjugation by

    confronting submission,
    negotiating independence,
    (with fearful heart).

Resolute mind stood firm
refusing to be a casualty
without being dead.

— ❧ —

Audacity

(Always) hungry for approval,

    looking for consent,
    neglecting dignity and grace,
    surrendering battles with no regrets,
    tolerating unfair restraints
    while yearning for freedom in confinement.

    Accepting bread of resentment,
    enduring pain of worthlessness
    time and again.
    Meeting life meekly,
    avoiding looking straight into its eyes,
    I waited for daunting directions.

Overwhelmed by cowardly behavior:
    no resistance to tender,
    no shelter to hide
    (from dominance),

I was left to survive, with captivity gained from ignorance,
until I joined hands with audacity, and
learned to stand my ground firm.

Subsequent to long struggle, (gradually)
Boldness assuages attacks on emotions,
Restraints begin to emancipate,
Consents not abided,
Approvals not needed.

Battered sentiments mended steadily,
Battles conquered,
Silence conversed,
Heart and soul rescued,
Conscience delivered, and
Freedom consummated.

— ❧ —

Bypassing Rules

Bypassing rules of absolute obedience,
liberating my existence,
energizing my heart,
I desired to reclaim life
by neglecting the past, and
welcoming the present with my mind.

> Dreaming state of
>   relaxation,
> endeavoring departure from
>   self-imposed silence,
> struggling to attain
>   self-reliance,
> I sought out the precious jewel of independence
>   by paying attention to my heart.

Assembling ego and spirit apart,
wrapping confined past,
navigating boat of
new resolutions
on waters of
self-determination,
I managed to move towards the
tempting shores of liberation.

— ೲ —

A Mind at Peace

Done with sorrow,
done with grief,
blessed with joy,
blessed with relief,

> heart full of red life,
> mind void of ambiguity,
> (whether awake, or asleep),
> warm solace accompanies me.

Disturbed past—my History,
Comforting present—my Victory,
Cheerful days—my Serenity,
Peaceful nights—my Ecstasy,
Pleasant future—my Destiny.

> A mind at peace is
> richer than a crown.
> Heart relishes in comfort,
> moments of peacefulness
> deliver joy to my journey.

After leaving icy tomb of silence,
I realize the secret of happy survival

> love begins life,
> awareness delivers power,
> forgiveness brings comfort.
> Never shall I succumb to my fate
> like a battle-worn flag of surrender.

— ෙ —

Sweet Memories

Diluting sweet memories in
           dismal thoughts,
welcoming happiness with
           genuine heart,
providing pleasure
           chance to survive,
I patiently walked
           lengthy bridge of time
giving myself a delightful opportunity
           to enjoy, leisurely, every sip of life.

— ❧ —

Cold Winds of Helplessness

Customs and traditions wear me numb
    leaving me like an offender
        in confinement, or
            a cat without self-reliance,
                unable to resist total submission.

Storm brews inside my mind
    turning brain into slush of snow and ice;
        cold winds of helplessness
            freeze corridors of my mind.
                My troubled soul searches
                    for warmth of emancipation.

I request comfort to resurface on ice, and
    for departed calm to return to its abandoned site.

— ❧ —

Journey from Confinement to Freedom

We never shared our hearts,
we never spoke our minds,
our dreams were different,
our miseries were private,
our cups of patience were full,
our barrel of love was empty,
our partnership was a confusion.

    Two strangers emotionally unaccompanied,
    existed together in different hemispheres.

Precious years of youth,
wrapped in thickest sheets of quiet,
kept me vigilant
for the slightest movement at bedside,
despite un-kept promises,
empty bed, and lonely nights.

    Bewildered, agitated,
    incarcerated, disintegrated,
    barely breathing,
    on the battleground of my life.

Turn of events—gray in agony,
required permanent solution.

I dissolved the painful union, and moved forward

    to restrain grief,
    to erase pain,
    to revive self-confidence,
    to call back my out-flown spirits,
    to gather withered leaves of my life, and
    to grow a healthy tree out of my wilted existence.

— ∾ —

Evenly Trapped

Free soul from a cosmopolitan city
with wings unclipped,
and a businessman from the countryside,
guardian of customs and traditions,
were brought together by conservative parents
for better and for worse.

East and west evenly trapped
in emotional confusion,
struggled to build lives with dissimilar temperaments.

Perturbed minds,
forcing calm outside with brewing storm inside,
were caught gasping in the sea of severe traditions
like a vessel trapped in alarming upheaval.

Gentleman from conservative family,
felt his authority under siege and
his sovereignty threatened.

The lady from liberal surroundings,
was desperate to hold on to silver strings
of her meagre allowance of freedom.

Living on enormously different wavelengths,
they existed together at wits' end,
yearning for each other's attention.

As distance widened,
aloneness befriended the couple permanently
heading them towards the cliff of severance.

Cloaked with anxiety,
    they searched for a feasible remedy
    to solve chronic problem of aloneness,
    like doctors contemplating probable treatment
    for a terminal patient's progressively deteriorating state.

To keep their partnership intact,
the couple strove to turn the fall of their susceptible union
into fragrant spring of their lives.

Finally they realized,

    their vulnerable plant of alliance
    needed soil of open communication.

    Efforts to make compromise
    brought them to a reasonable solution.

Authority and sovereignty behaved reasonably:

    privileges were not relinquished completely,
    freedom survived, partially.

Consignment of New Ambitions

Unsettled feelings whirled like a wrecked ship
making mortal miles difficult to negotiate.

> Sorrows and regrets, without shore,
> floated in stream of consciousness,
> mounting discomfort in turbulent mind.

Averting strong waves of disturbing thoughts,
pursuing calm waters of life,

> I attempted to unload the cargo
> of slaughtered hopes and shattered dreams,
> to make room
> for the consignment of new ambitions
> with renewed vision.

— ❧ —

Fragile Sanity

Trapped nervously in silent thoughts,
    anxious behind a protective mask,
        apprehensive to rebel against rules of compliance,
      I took refuge in superficial calm
        considering it my safe heaven.

After trading mind and soul
    to appease people around me,
      I tried (in vain),

        to seek out strength in my neglected self, and
        searched comfort in immense discomfort.

Demon of affliction
    made susceptible sanity shrill for mercy
      making silence too loud to comprehend.

Perpetual restlessness shook me awake,
    forced my deprived self to call for boldness
      to take concrete measures
        against unreasonable compromises,
          and to unshackle subdued existence
        from noxious pressure.

— ❧ —

Golden Dreams

I was one hell of a dreamer
    of sweet dreams
holding on silently
    to precious thoughts,
trying relentlessly
    for prized ambitions.

Watching drifts of wind,
    patiently,
I stood firm and waited
    for barriers of confiscated choices
        to be removed.

Golden dreams do not disperse
in the face of difficulties,

hopes, solid as a thick wall of stone,
cannot be shaken with gusty winds.

With un-hurrying chase,
with unshaken faith,

    I waited, optimistically,
    to be rewarded by imperial treasure.

— ❧ —

Robbers

Those robbed
    of precious integrity and individuality,
being convinced to negotiate
    anger and pain
        embracing clemency!

Had integrity and individuality been ensured
of resumption of honor and respect?

Had culprits been reprimanded
and convinced not to repeat their mistakes?

or

Is it a new trap for innocents
to fall a prey once again?

— ❧ —

Heavenly Intervention

Desires
    clouded by fog of frustration,
Talents
    eclipsed with rejection,
Dreams
    vanished in disappointment,
Hopes
    melted like fragile flakes of snow.

Stewing in anxiety,
holding knapsack of dejection,
fatigued with uphill struggle,

    I survived with restless mind and drained body.

Exhausted, searching for valor and strength,
I asked for Heavenly intervention.

    Blissful gift of insight opened my eyes:

Desires
    could be exhilarated by leaving despair behind,
Talents
    could be awakened by paying attention to heart and mind,
Dreams
    could be revived with the energy of relaxation,
Hopes
    could be resuscitated back to life.

— ❧ —

When My Brain is Lost

When my brain is lost
in the middle of a hasty storm,

and its precious silence takes leave
for stretches of time,

drums of fear beat aloud,
generating fatigue of mind,

strong pillars of sanity
are left brittle and worn,

restless heart beats faster
to weather the storm.

Horror of confusion and loss
stays days after the storm subsides.

Search for quiet is launched
in the middle of thunder and lightning,

sails are spread to request
the vessel of silence to stay around;

drifted ship has to be harbored back
with all my senses intact.

— ॐ —

Icy Rock of Grievances

Murky clouds of apprehension
overshadowed life,

agitated soul,
inflamed with suppression,
sliced through my existence,

depository of unhappy memories,
inhaled anxiety,

aching heart,
robbed of life from my eyes,

ignorance provided courage
to trap excruciating anger inside,

sadness threatened frail sanity,
helplessness caused resentment.

Hope was the vantage point
that kept me
above the tidal wave of desperation.

My search for autonomy never exhausted;
quest for resolution gained momentum.

I called for Providential advice.

After lifetime of patience,
I vowed to deal with life audaciously.

Inner calm abandoned anxiety steadily,
icy rock of grievances melted gradually,
fury and frustration were forced to back off.

Little by little (my) soul learned
to blossom with relaxation.

My worn-out life rejuvenated
with confidence and vitality.

Ignorance

Accepting defeat before combating,
      a mistake,

conceding power before challenging,
      ignorance,

silence before vocalizing concerns,
      a limitation,

holding grievances before clarification,
      a blunder,

dwelling in assumptions
before looking for reality,
      a failure,

yearning to cast off baggage
without endeavoring,
      a fantasy.

— ❧ —

Intelligence

Reclaiming lost identity,
                    bravery,

acknowledging true feelings,
                    honesty,

connecting with reality,
                    insight,

endeavoring to be rid of old baggage,
                    courage,

vocalizing concerns before being silent,
                    wisdom,

accomplishing independence,
    to set mind and spirits
        free,
                    intelligence.

— ❧ —

Renewed Tune of Insight

When obstacles in life require
insight,
problems call forth for
patience,
adversities start to
instruct,
mind concentrates on deserting
anxiety;

it endeavors to find
harmony,
and strives to
abandon
upheavals and uncertainties.

Different chemistry
plays liberating part:

serenity
makes to weary heart,

inner peace
rekindles blurred track of consciousness

diverting nomadic mind
towards domains of reality and intellect.

Transformed intelligence,
      hums happily
focusing on
      varied options and multitude of possibilities

      with diverse chemistry,
      with dynamic substance,
      with passion and conviction
      composing symphony of life
      with renewed tune of insight.

Shore of Emancipation

Accommodating
    self-assurance,
welcoming
    state of acceptance,
neglecting
    rules of constraints,
I paid attention to my heart.

Taking stronger grip on
    restricted state,
I signed up to
    transform,
hoping to pave way for
    self-determination.

Welcoming
    constructive suggestions,
navigating boat of
    autonomous decisions,
turning towards
    optimistic direction,

I endeavored to paddle
    the canoe of hopes and expectations
towards
    the shore of emancipation.

— ❧ —

Taj Mahal

Ears waited for
        warm words,
desires hungered for
        affection,
heart longed to
        belong,
no one built a Castle of Love for me.

Holding my world
        together
I existed without a
        pulse
before awareness ripped
        the shroud of distress.

Eventually, I realized

love, like a coin,
        contains two sides;

receiving and delivering
        do not differ in
        significance.

I constructed Taj Mahal around me
    without waiting for someone else
        to begin building the monument of love.

— ❦ —

Valiant Façade

Living with valiant façade,
subsequent to
confiscated rights and
ignored talents,
feels
like existing without
Heaven's Blessings.

    Darkness expands her domain,
    winds of desperation fly away spirits
    making her feel helpless
    like a bird with clipped wings
    in an open door prison.

Confinement
    throbs in veins,
    happiness seems
    a fantasy,
    life becomes
    a breathing casualty.

Heart, with no ease,
    torn in strips,
    looks for mending.

Self-esteem and pride
    plead to be
    rescued.

Inflamed emotions
    request for
    immediate attention.

At that moment,
    if pain is fed on
    hope,
    ultimately
    optimism
    shows path to
    deliverance.

Fear and vulnerability
    hide their ugly faces
    in disappointment,

life empties her bowl of
    bitterness
    to its last drop,

refilling it with
    happiness and
    sending invitation to
    harmony and tranquility
    to embrace
    troubled existence.

— ಸಿ —

Virtues and Vices

A desperate soul,
    poised and calm, but confident and strong,
    mind full of positive thoughts and future plans,
    made decisions, fulfilled her mission
    with concealed determination, with firm resolution.

Dreading confrontation
                every moment,
like a frightened sheep among
                hungry lions.

She availed herself of a chance for her younger generation
    to nurture their minds,
    to liberate their innocent souls.

Fulfilled with accomplishment,
determined to realize a dream of her youth,

she came back to school
    to nourish her mind,
        to invigorate her life.

As shadows of unawareness receded,
enlightenment splintered values of her past,
like an enormous blow would shatter a thick glass.

Her Virtues:
    surrendering to unconditional obedience,
    keeping zero vocabulary for words of defiance;

    accepting unfair conditions with no resistance,
    like a weak structure under catastrophic conditions,

    once considered medals of honor,
    turned out to be
    cowardly actions and awards of ignorance.

Bewildered,
    perplexed,
        shaken and
            lost,

hesitant to differentiate right from wrong,
desiring ambiguity to be resolved,
she craved shelter for her transformed thoughts.

The girl realized:

    staying involved in contrary thoughts,
    would exhaust her strength,
    weaken her purpose.

The desperate soul strove to come out of uncertainty
    with emotions settled,
    with confidence restored.

— ⸙ —

Symphony of Love

Ignorance is a burden on
                    human race,
suppression results in a
                    repulsive state.

Knot was tied in heaven,
decision was made on earth
                    by ignorant parents.

Their verdict broke
                    two affectionate hearts,
like a carelessly handled crystal vase.

Bride and bridegroom were left
                    option less,
wading the sea
                    of vulnerability.
Push of shock damaged
                    previously occupied hearts
like stormy winds
                    tatter sails of a yacht.

Pierced with grief, bride and bridegroom,
                    reluctantly,
joined their hands to breed
                    the shrub of their lives
with misplaced seeds,
with painful endeavor.

They concealed anguish,
disciplined sorrows,

distressed under
mutual regrets,

fumbled at their spirits,
like amateurs at piano keys.

Two flowers bloomed
in their wilted plant,
          but
rocks underneath
stayed firm.

As years advanced
the couple overlooked
their union's gloomy side,

combined authenticity
altered two unhappy hearts,

sapphire of fidelity and jewel of trust,
brought them together.

Balm of loyalty restored
abrasions of once bruised hearts.

Music merged in its notes,
liberated souls played symphony of love;

gem of mutual affection
set in their wedding rings.

— ❧ —

Gender Disparity

Self-esteem, self-confidence, self-reliance, and feelings of wholeness are casualties of gender disparity.

The Secret of Tranquility

Yielding desires and ambitions
                sadly,
signing against self-reliance
                unhappily,
accommodating desperation
                permanently,
I relied on knotty patience
                patiently.

Domiciling in tender state
                continually,
floating with clouds of anxiety
                constantly,
(because of society's
                gender disparity),
I stayed in agony
                ceaselessly.

After a lifetime of emotional upheaval,
    I summoned courage
        to unravel the secret of tranquility:

I had to confront
    the demon of gender disparity
        to obtain my rightful place in society.

— ❧ —

Sacrificial Lamb

Ebony eyes on rosy face,
willowy body, covered with shreds,
bare feet walking on icy streets,
product of poverty in
Swat Valley, Pakistan,

flourished in beauty,
thrived in multiple miseries.

Fifteen year old,
timid like a wood dove,
    with throbbing heart,
    with secret thoughts,
    with sunny smiles,
    with grazing eyes,

unaware of her parents' grievous state,
ignorant of her afflicted fate,
dreaming to tread on the wings of breeze,
stepped swiftly into puberty.

    During the dark of night,
    the landlord received gift of his choice.

Her father's debts were paid,
her brothers were saved from starvation,
family's unfertile land was spared and
hunger was beaten for one more year.

Innocence lost,
eyes down cast,
haunted looks,
slaughtered dreams,
liveliness washed in
funereal silence, after
crossing the waters of disgrace.

On unstable feet
with her shaky subsistence,
fifteen year old,
sneaked into her house,
before tears of dew dried.

— ❧ —

The Bride

Swelled with tension,
heavy with apprehension,
carrying her husband's baby in her womb,
expectant mother
never spoke her dreads aloud.

After giving birth to a
healthy female child,
she emptied her flooded eyes,
"as horizon clears its
moisture of black clouds."

Embarrassed
about her own flesh and blood,
consumed with distress,
attired in shroud of shame,
the mother faced family
like someone condemned.

Sweeping gray ashes of anguish aside,
she stepped out from canopy of grief, and
vowed to her infuriated man
to deliver bundle of his lost glory—
A Son,
when he begets her pregnant again.

Little girl's survival
was no one's concern.
she was a sour in her father's eye,
and the heaviest burden
on his shoulders to abide.

Her doom was written
before her descent:

destined to be someone's bride,
after the age of nine,
she had to wait for puberty
to become her bridegroom's wife;

nonetheless, she was available for his delights.

The discarded doll of rag,
from cradle to grave,
was never welcomed, always crazed.

She dwelled in infringing heat of
    insecurity,
growing up in the house of
    humiliation,
enduring chronic disease of
    inferiority;

living with abundance of fear and disgrace,
    she was another casualty
        of South Asian females' fate.

Resurrection

*Prolonged recovery from
life-threatening conditions
sometimes amounts to a
second chance at life.*

Sometimes Asleep, Others Awake

Suds
    Suds
        Suds

An upright leg
    Being
        Washed...
Yellowish
    Suds
        Perfectly
Absorbed
    in Green Cloth...

Hallucination...
    Confusion...
        Hallucination...

Classroom?
    Noisy students
        (with Professor)?

Mechanic's workshop?
    Master mechanic
        (with Workers)?

Anesthesia-induced state...
    Sometime asleep...
        Others awake...

Eyes
    (wide Open)
        See surroundings
            (without Face)

Colorless Shades
        Formless Shapes

Ears
        (full of Noise)
                Too feeble
                        to grasp,

Hazy mind
        (cannot comprehend)
                Neither fully Alive…
                        Nor completely dead

Confusion…
        Confusion…
                Confusion,

Out of Body Experience!
        Angels
                (in familiar outfits)

Talking
        Laughing,
                Working (Diligently)

Sounds
        (of surgical apparatus)
                Chainsaw
                      Hammer
                          Chisel
                              Clink!…

Then…Nestling…
Comfortably…
Leisurely…
Hazily…

Struggling…
(to comprehend)
Upheaval
Activity
Around me.

Familiar Voice—
Familiar Words—
Beautiful!…Fantastic!…It's Done!

Dr. Rumble's triumphant Face
(I See)—

He has accomplished—
A (brand new) Knee!

Altered image
(of Operation Theater)
Destroyed Sanctity
Shattered Solemnity.

Later…Recovery
(on Orthopedic Floor).

Smiles of Encouragement
Hands so Proficient

Convince my endurance
       (to allow)
            Rigorous Therapy
                 (to establish)
                       Maximum Mobility

     In

        My

           Young

             Knee…

(October 2009 – Knee surgery, with spinal anesthesia)

— ❧ —

Grimful Glee or Total Victory

perplexed...bewildered...disoriented...

eccentric site—
strange venue—

ambiguous...confusing...

memories retired from
pure light to dark night
things harbored in mind
slipped away one by one
neglecting obedience
closing door behind
as though leaving eternally
abandoning me to encounter
out of body experience

obscurity...oblivion...obscurity
fatigue...languor...exhaustion

images emerging
images drifting
constantly

was I alive!
was I dead!
was it my room!
was it an unfamiliar place?

memory struggled
like a sinking swimmer
in turbulent sea.

I closed my eyes—
I tried to open locked door
without slaughtering my hope,
without knowing what to expect.

I struggled to know how to cope
having journeyed to oblivion.

Was I back?

gradually drifting thoughts regressed,
clashing to find their original place,
memories struggled to refresh,

with my traits,
with my alertness—
separated from rust,
returned to their nest

was a blessing—
was a grace—
nothing was taken back.

I was invigorated with
all my senses intact,

no diminished traits—
no postponed intellect—
few dizzy spells,
guest for few days—
the Bargain was the Best.

Before my dust was put
to an empty urn,

I took a backward step—
into my domain.

(2010 – My mini stroke)

— ❧ —

At the Mercy of a Craftsman

I slept anesthetic sleep quite a few times,
*   during childhood, youth and maturity*
tonsillectomy, spinal-fusion, and
*   total replacement of knees.*

On operating table,
motionless like a still pebble,
detached from universe,
slightly risen from the dead,

under highly proficient hands,
expressionless like a wall of stone,
at the mercy of a craftsman,
I spend hours closer to eternity,

I come back, half-alive, from surgery.

After anesthesia wears off,
I wake up from celestial sleep,
experiencing hammering pain
in my replaced knee.

I lie moaning wishing for the state,
when presence and absence make no difference.

Emotions run beyond forbearance,
valor withers like flowers in blazing sun;

easel of my existence,
(painted with colors of agony)
seems to cringe under my hazy, misty eyes.

I care little about the candle of my life.
Days and nights, spent in torment,
before ray of relief leads my slow walk on
the road to recovery.

— ॐ —

Brutal Encounter

Mothers, lifeless,
searching for their lost soul,
vanish in abyss of grief
should they lose a child.

My youngest son endures
assault on his vibrant heart
under the eyes of moon and stars.

Little ones,
asleep in comfortable beds,
awaken by ambulance—screaming,
watch their father carried away from home.

Young wife,
dreading worst from hospital,
pacing in agony like
a prisoner, conscious of innocence,
awaits capital punishment.

Brutal encounter devastates a jovial family
as an atrocious earthquake
shakes a well-established home.

Fearful wife's anguish shatters the earth,
stature of her pain touches heaven
as helplessness makes it to the Utmost Authority,
the young life is revived back to recuperate.

(August 2007)

— ❧ —

Resurrection

After replacement of a diseased knee,
    to proceed without complexities,
        I served time, in a facility, with varied felons.

    Ten days sufficient for comrades in custody,
    twenty-four days mandatory for my captivity.

To state motives for my longer detention,
charges delivered by my surgeon, Dr. Bhupathi:

cardiac arrest—my vulnerability,
    formation of blood clot—a possibility,
        prescription narcotics—professional custody.
            To endure severity of extensive therapy—
                a prerequisite for graduation from the facility;

to avert fatal tragedy,
    to keep from bleeding intensely,
        until assigned time fulfilled completely,
            round the clock vigil—a necessity.

After completing the term of detention,
I was sent home
    with heavy dosages of medications, and
    strict regime of exercises
    to apprehend normal movement of renewed knee.

    Anxiety slashed through my soul,
    cruel hand of annoying pain, misplaced my faith,
    deserting activities of life, was an immense sentence.

One morning,
    before the birds, before the sun engulfed the world,
    I woke up and requested audacity to take a bold step.
    Subsequent to immense struggle,
    I managed to leave my nest for the bookstore.

Sitting by the window,
    indifferent to books and magazines,
        I engaged myself in spectacles on the street.

Exuberance was in the air:
    rows of elegant trees,
        drenched in opulent gold,
            attired in full green,
                stood across the street.

Cars and buses raced
    like horses of different breeds,
        children dressed in smiles,
            walked towards their schools.

Young and old,
    vigorously, moved along the street;
        some waved for taxis, others preferred buses
            for their commute.

Vitality resurrected
   My spirits,
      Hope rocked me in
         Her gentle arms,
           And
             Set
               Me
                 Free.

— ॐ —

Restored Gift

My first born
taken to the operation theater
for forty minutes of minor procedure,
was brought back on a gurney,
after acutely perilous, six and a half hours
of intensely complicated and extremely strenuous
heart repair,
into the hands of commitment.

My son,
with a new valve,
with a triple bypass,
attached to a ventilator,
motionless like a sacrificed lamb,
concealed in tubes and IVs,
bleeding profusely,

surviving—without living
unaware of surroundings,
oblivious of sufferings,
contributing no efforts for resurgence
like a drowning novice swimmer
sinking ferociously in a deep ocean.

The loved ones deeply cut in heart,
with pain bright, with fears raw,
waited anxiously
to be saved from a brutal calamity.

A young life—on the verge of nothingness,
was brought back from the claws of eternity.
A prey was diligently rescued from jaws of a fierce beast.
Merciful hand secured a son, a brother, and a husband.

(April 2008)

— ॐ —

Health

A blessing—once lost, no amount of regret can charm it back.

Health

Health is a blessing from God.
One who loses it
feels helpless and lost.

When fear dwells in heart,
and strength starts to part,
it helps to do away with blues.

False hopes and excuses—
colorful barriers,
encumber course of fitness.

Move sincerely towards
patience and persistence—
solid pillars of strength.

Reset your priorities,
rewrite your rules,
walk hand in hand with
intellect and gathered sense
to obtain a new lease on your health;

inch miles of life
with professional guidance,
with personal ambitions, and
with candid determination,
like a proficient student.

— ❧ —

Ready to Negotiate

My years' long acquaintance with
    throbbing pain
was as strong as a bond of friendship
    between two friends.

Life changed with
    scarcity of health,
    deterioration in strength, and
    limitation of movement.

Captive body controlled by
    abundance of constraints,
    confiscated pleasures, and
    unleashed torments.

On the flip side, blessed with
    independent soul,
    mental freedom,
    wealth of confidence,
    affluence of patience, and
    unshaken determination.

Acknowledging blessings,
ignoring calamities,
accepting limitations,
neglecting tumultuous storm of discontents,
fighting against life of physical chains,
accommodating what fate revealed,
combating with every fiber of my strength,
struggling out of my bed each morning.

I was

    always

        ready

            to

                negotiate

                    a new day.

— ❧ —

Sweaty Terror

Excruciating pain,
when like a companion,
you visit me time and again,

my wit is in peril
like a kidnapped train,

valor in danger
like someone caught in a hurricane,

alertness in jeopardy
like memory trapped in aged brain.

Your persistent company drains strength,
vulnerability wears out my existence,
sweaty terror fills mind,
toxic anxiety grips heart.
I moan helplessly under your passion,
neglecting singing birds,
ignoring blossoming summer and
forgetting sweet dreams.

I search for relief.

Your crimson affection like furious rage,
leaves me trembling inside
as though I've escaped, narrowly,
from my own pearl harbor.

I've overpaid your debts
with ten years of my youth.

Stop claiming so much of me,

try not to pull the plug
on my fragile existence.

— ဆ —

Underwritten Existence

"Scenery of adulthood was not scenic:
my lute broken and tune muted,"
tears evident in smiles,
helplessness apparent in patience.

    Persecuted by anguish,
    deserted by comfort,
    well versed in aches and pains
    like a person seasoned in love and passion.

Detained freedom,
constrained endurance,
weathered by sufferings
of a chastised prisoner,
death in life, survival in torment.

Why did You underwrite my existence?
How far should I carry the baggage of ill health?
Hadn't I accomplished enough misery?
When would I walk with vigor and strength?

I had accepted the agonized ordeal with no argument,
hoping tomorrow's sun would greet me
with blessings of a new beginning:

    sufferings erased,
    health restored and
    body spared from paralyzing pain.

— ➷ —

Migration

Mostly a well-thought out and calculated decision, but sometimes unavoidable circumstances also call for it. Either way it yields bittersweet experiences.

Jewel of Freedom

A little girl of seven,
unaware of
prejudice, hate, and discrimination
against any race or religion,
sharing culture, and breathing space
with multi-racial associates,
lived in undivided India, prior to
August fourteen, nineteen forty seven.

A swift change of events
disarrayed her existence,
like Katrina disheveled New Orleans.

Fire of anxiety,
smoke of fear,
disturbed feeling of security,
distressed peace of mind.

Firearms perturbed the atmosphere.
Belongings plundered,
properties blazed,
houses razed to the ground.

Young and old,
bewildered and defenseless,
searched for shelter
from immense violence.

Brutality reigned all over—
children killed,
adults murdered,
unborn babies
snatched
from bellies of young mothers,
girls raped,
boys kidnapped,
young brides separated from their
beloved husbands,
old spouses vanished
without a trace,
children desperate for parents,
parents frantic for missing children,
elderly and sick denied assistance.

Infants died in distress,
were assigned
shallow graves
for permanent residences
without courtesy of
shrouds or flowers.

Battered ones longed for
salvation
during emergence of
the Independent State of
Pakistan.

The little girl lost in chaos,
anxious and confused,
accompanied with fear,
found herself on a truck.

She ended up in a refugee camp
with her mother,
without a trace of
her beloved father.

No house to live in,
no bed to sleep,
nothing to eat,
muddy water to drink.

Getting into a shower—
a fantasy,
protection against violence—
an impossibility.

Spending days under a tent
in scorching heat,
preceded by
torrential rains.

The little girl survived
among demons and friends.

Innocence lost,
childhood gone astray,
walking trail of sufferings,
searching for lost utopia,
waiting for her father
anxiously.

Her mother,
haunted by husband's absence,
dressed in silence,
covered with woe,
sat emotionally exhausted
with reservoirs of strength low,
with levels of adversities elevated.

Engulfed in grief,
filled bottle of hope
with despair,
washed her face
with tears,
with restless heart,
with vacant eyes,
waited for news of her
missing husband.

The enormity of miseries
swelled high,
the ditch of helplessness
grew deep,
before
she heard the approaching footsteps of
her beloved one.

Uncertainty jarred her existence,
she lurched between
hope and disbelief.

Finally,
fog of desperation faded,
glory of the moment brightened,
a smile rose to illuminate her face.

Happiness encircled
desperate souls,
merciful heaven
showered
blessings on them,
the family was
together once again.

Endeavoring to ignore
memories of separation and loss,
the family tried to reconcile
with hurtful past.

They celebrated
reunion
with buoyant hearts,
accepting
hefty price of the
Coveted Jewel of Freedom.

— ❧ —

Moving from New York

Facing migration to a foreign land
    for the sake of my grandchildren, was
        a firm decision,
            a pleasurable choice, and
                a colossal challenge.

When the moment arrived to move to Toronto,
    a place dissimilar to New York,
        apprehensions were caught
            too close to my heart.

Defying sentiments was a difficult task,
    ignoring precious memories a great loss,
        leaving family, friends, and mentors,
            felt like breaking a promise,
                or refusing a shot of sacramental wine.

Farewell to a place
    that became my own cherished space—
        where I learned to walk light with grace,
        where I realized to live with
            endurance and smiles combined,

where determination overwhelmed fears,
    where opportunities balanced obstacles,
        where purpose flavored life,
            where seeds of forgiveness
                were sown in my ignorant mind
                    to free my grave heart,
                        to restore my perturbed soul.

To move from my beloved city
   with a brave face, and
      to celebrate my new space,

Pandora's box of contrary thoughts had to be closed,
     map of unfinished dreams not to be erased,
        sanctity of each cathedral to be acknowledged, as
           life could not to be journeyed on a three-legged horse.

To accomplish transition, effectively,
    from New York to Toronto,
      with an open heart,
       with a clear mind,
        with no reservation,
         to move forward, and
          adopt a new soil,

efforts to be placed
   (concurrently)
      to find a common place
        for chronicles to store,
          for new dreams to generate,
            for new promises to seize.

— ❧ —

Argue Not

Power of serendipity,
figment of imagination—
crystal-clear invitation
to revelations and miracles.

Dreams of future,
power of insight,
pillars of self-assurance and
foundation of a new beginning.

    Argue not for limitations,
    regret not for leaving comforts behind.
    Migration is not end of successful mission,
    changed venues do not confine talents.

    They emit colossal challenges,
    present enormous occasions,
    expand capabilities,
    enhance horizon.

Creation and destruction,
sacrifice and longing—
naked truth of nature,
collaborate purpose, promote life.

    Impediments and failures,
    unlock doors of new enterprises,
    increase endurance, renew passion,
    generate enormous perception,
    energize efforts towards destination.

Explore through constructive avenues of mind
    with massive energy
    with gigantic ambition.

    Commence a new journey,
    resume a sturdy footing,
    envision the sky a limit.

    Secret of significant survival:
    precise judgment, and
    unyielding commitment.

— ॐ —

Family

An important institution—provides nourishment to the family tree that bears healthy fruits of love, care, and protection, and imparts sense of belonging.

My Family by My Side

When larks and sparrows
    announce a day,
When morning light
    brightens my way,
When pleasure and enjoyment
    beget joy beyond measure,
When breezes sing
    a melodious song,
When fragrant flowers
    bloom all around, and
Heaven showers
    blessings down,
When sun shines
    in full glory,
When moon and stars
    mesmerize my soul,
When night captivates
    every delight,
Moments pronounce:
    My Family by My Side.

— ৯ —

A Window in My Past

Train of my thoughts runs on track
of heart-warming memories.
Its final destination is
State of Jovial Pleasure—
my two adorable grandchildren.

I open a window in my past,
happiness runs in me like red blood,
spirits resonate melody in delight.

I visualize:

Three little boys
growing up in our happy habitat;
school bus full of vibrant children,
brings them to realm of
knowledge and intellect.

Back at home, three energetic ones,
after finishing homework
spend leisure time with friends
playing in the neighborhood park.

Under parents' vigilant eyes,
they amble into adulthood
as self-assured conscientious individuals.

Three young men leave for further studies,
establish themselves overseas
with their beloved spouses.

Once again we are together,
surrounded by happiness and unlimited blessings.

I welcome new stars in our constellation

with heart and soul,
with limitless treasure,
with immense pleasure,
dawn of our new generation—
my two grandchildren.

I behold once again, familiar pattern with pride:

Little ones,
on the road of knowledge and intelligence,
under parental supervision.

With beautiful shades of past and present
life comes full circle for our happy habitat.

— ❧ —

A Spring-like Day In Autumn

When you arrived my little one
your innocent face made me realize,
how people must feel mesmerized in Heaven!

    Your presence—
    a reminder of spring in fragrance,
    in a blooming garden
    in the early April morning.

Dressed in loose outfit, in my backyard,
strolling serenely looking for a spot
to collect thoughts and enjoy
a spring-like day in autumn,

    when sun deserted gusty winds,
    when haze abandoned horizon,
    when rain strayed away to honor
    tranquil pleasure of the day,
    when smothering heat and freezing cold,
    disowned serene moments,
    when nature spread out rainbow on dry ground,

        magic seized my breath.

I sat humming on thinly spread multicolored sheet,
    absorbed in my thoughts,
    visualizing a young woman
    waiting for a new arrival.

Would she be blessed with a boy or a girl?

    Happily she realized
    God's splendor would suffice.

A Healthy Child
    was her Only Concern.

— ❧ —

Our Little Angel

After a long fearful night,
threatened by weakening heartbeat
of an unborn child,
witnessing young mother suffer
thirty hours of agonizing labor,
ship of my hope anchored in the Bay of Mercy.

As darkness launched her boat away,
early morning hours celebrated
first cry of an innocent life;

our constellation welcomed a new star,
my granddaughter, Zainab, was born.

Anwar and Alina (on cloud nine)
celebrated arrival of their first child.

Our hearts filled with gratitude, offered thanks
for the exquisite blessing from Gracious God.

Our healthy little girl,
apple of our eyes,
serenity of our hearts,
fountain of our delights,
brilliance of our universe
was a colossal blessing from Almighty God.

— ๑ —

The Perfect Creation

A candle was lit,
a wish was made,
a prayer was said,
a little girl was welcomed,
Shamsis and Dossals were blessed
with a gift of new life.

    Bells of joy were heard,
    notes of congratulations were read,
    bouquets of love were prepared,
    from life's dawn, happiness was drawn.
    So great a glory did the parents confer.

Thick velvety hair
crowned beautiful face,
captive ebony eyes
mesmerized our universe,
precious smiles, and
little cries of protest
thrilled us all.

    Thanks were offered the day we were blessed
    with our beloved granddaughter, Zainab—
    a perfect creation of God earned our hearts.

— ❧ —

A Gift from Heaven

On wings of early morning hours,
a precious gift of unfathomable pleasure
was delivered from Heaven:

Alina and Anwar
were honored with a healthy child.

    Shamsis and Dossals
    were blessed with a precious grandson,
    on January 26, two thousand five.

Candles of happiness,
prepared with wax of pride,
threaded with wick of delight,
were lit to offer thanks
to Benevolent Authority
on safe arrival of baby boy, Nabeel.

    Aroma of delight
    covered every corner of our blessed house,
    carols of thanks were sung
    to acknowledge Providence's grace.

Radiant sun and white sheets of snow,
shared celebrations with proud parents, and
their cherished daughter, Zainab.

— ❦ —

My Precious Grandchildren

When you grace my space,
   time holds its breath,
      happiness revives,
         pleasure comes alive,
            innocence triumphs,
               moments rejoice.

Glimmer in your eyes
   matches stars on a clear dark sky,
      your charming ecstatic faces,
      your captivating smiles
         bring rainbow to the ground.

Earth stays still under
   your soft feet
      like freshly fallen snow on streets,
         buds of happiness blossom all around,
            my jubilant heart commemorates
         happy occasion.

Warmth in abundance
   summer in permanence
      proclaim
         my precious grandchildren's
         greatly blessed presence.

— ❧ —

Contentment

The affinity I feel,
    the happiness I relish,
the pleasure I accumulate,
    the satisfaction I experience,
the innocence I witness,
    the love I receive
from my grandchildren,
    equips me
with purpose and contentment.

— ❧ —

Glorious Moments

"Morning rain foretells a pleasant day,
showers of happiness melt ice of dismay."

Days full of glorious moments
    arrive into stillness of my life,
rainbow of pleasure
    conquers my heart,
heavenly bliss
    surrounds me with gorgeous halo,

        when my grandchildren are with me.

Innocent faces
    sparkle with pleasure,
mischievous eyes
    twinkle with gleaming stars,
magical voices
    overflow with joy.

Their delightful manners, filled with affection,
    mesmerize my universe
    completing my blissful life.

— ☙ —

Two Beautiful Flowers

Before years were spent,
before journey was done,

time-worn tree of
my heavenly dreams,

bloomed with
two beautiful flowers,
Zainab and Nabeel.

My adorable grandchildren
carrying fragrance of love,

brought buckets full of sunshine,
to warm winter of my life.

The pleasurable past of my younger life,
invigorated with laughter and joy.

Happiness materialized
like golden rays on dark cloudy sky.

— ❧ —

Gratitude

I offer my thanks to Thee
    for the daughter never bestowed to me;
    depriving me of the pleasure was a blessing.
    Customs and traditions—the cargo,
    I could carry just for me,
    my little angel could have surrendered her vanity.

I offer my thanks to Thee
    for Three Flowers that bloomed in me—
    a source of merriment and delight,
    their fragrance enough to inebriate me.

I offer my thanks to Thee
    for the sense to protect my children's integrity,
    for providing strength to defy odds against them,
    for harmony, and for love I carry for them.

I offer my thanks to Thee
    for granting precious gifts to me—
    three adorable girls,
    loves of my sons,
    comforts of their souls,
    treasures to cherish,
    pleasures to sustain,
    for them and for me.

— ❦ —

A Sunflower at its Glorious Height

My Granddaughter Zainab, from Canada,
visited me in New York
during a snowy week of December,
accompanying warmth of pleasure,
turning snow and ice into blooming delight.

Her captivating presence,
    adorable gift,
        valuable present,

her sunny face,
    a sunflower
        at its glorious height,

her shining ebony eyes,
    a treat for sight,

her entertaining laughter,
    melody for ears,

her engaging talks,
    ecstasy for heart,

her healthy happy existence,
    blessing for my soul.

End of her trip was
    a challenging part
        for my melting heart;

with watery eyes,
    with lump in throat,
        forcing smile on my dismal face,

praying silently for
    her safety and health,

        I bade my Little Angel a
            goodbye
        as she left warmth
            of my hands
        for comforting arms of
            her parents.

— ✿ —

Stilled Forever

After I'm stilled forever,
 my loved ones,
  please, do not be sad.

 You've played
  absolutely vital role
   in honoring my life
    with contentment and comfort.

 Your love and care—sources of
  serenity and tranquility,
   have provided me strength
    during time of vulnerabilities.

I'll rest in peace
 with everlasting gratification
  as long as you'll be there
   for each other,
    in timely manner.

I've known God by his grace,
 behind calamities hide
  Providence's intelligence and
  Providential destinies;

  Sweetness replaces bitterness,
   roses do not lose charm
    living with thorns,
     if they maintain blooming face.

My treasured family together,
   helping each other
      in time of crisis,
         will fill my cold residence
           with comforting
              warmth and assurance,

           confirming
              I've performed
                 assigned (worldly) duties conscientiously.

— ᔆ —

Fabric of Support

Fabric of support by loved ones,
shields me against icy discomforts of life

like a densely knitted woolen jacket
protects me from frosty bites.

Fire of pleasure,
    ignites candle of joy,
    enlightens my enormously blessed existence,
    and keeps me intoxicated with contentment.

— ✺ —

Facts of Life

Crawling through experiences—
good and bad, happy and sad,
sweet and bitter, one develops
vision and insight to recognize
the facts of life.

Aloneness

Aloneness—

    a longing,
    a discomfort, and
    a frustration,

    involves more than
    a book,
    a piece of music, and
    a conversation.

    Blessed ones share
    companionship
    and communication.

Solitary stroll through avenues of mind—

    an adventure, and
    a pleasure, but
    no one to share thoughts—
    intellectual starvation.

A friend with depth and perception—

    a profound gift and
    a powerful source of
    mental ventilation,
    prevents
    cerebral suffocation.

— ✤ —

Invest In Beautiful Thoughts

Invest in beautiful thoughts,
ignite not misery of past,
listen to the language of pain,
honor your wounds swiftly.

Step outside of yourself,
tutor your pain
to negotiate the change,
let forgiveness be the comfort zone.

Foster not yesteryears' grudge,
heal through your heart,
keep detachment rapid and fast,
script your life anew
away from the agenda of past.

*(After listening to a chapter from a book by
Caroline Myss, I came up with this poem using
her words.)*

— ॐ —

Comfort Zone

Crossing threshold of
unsettled past,
acknowledge throbbing scars,
realize intensity of pain
to console your distressed self,

put away rosary of
bitter thoughts
to discipline grievances,
to minimize anxiety and loss.

Engrave exoneration
in your afflicted heart
to obtain gift of joyful mind.

Begin new phase of your life
generating a comfort zone
for productive thoughts.

(The message of Caroline Myss in my words)

— ❧ —

Capture the Moment

Capture the moment, savor the beauty,
let solace be your part.

Experience pleasure, enrich mind,
with consoling thoughts.

Let tender emotions surface;
short rainy season for eyes,
might dissolve ice of dismay
into warm pool of delight.

Peaceful heart,
    relishes in serenity,
    sings carol of happiness,
    celebrates life of fulfillment.

— ❧ —

Anger, Bitterness, Criticism

Anger:
Beast on a hill, serpent in a den,
product of rage, outcome of frustration,
splintered glass from shattered mirror
harmful for integrity and self-respect.

Bitterness:
Toxic for mind and body,
prescription for animosity,
ethical indecency begets perpetrator
morally and emotionally.

Criticism:
Blurred wisdom, immoral judgment,
colossal intrusion on personal freedom;
dark joy of manipulation
downright offensive, unpleasant and ugly.

— ଛ —

The Sweet Fruit of Patience

Warriors of ill fate,
live each day fiercely
with life and death combined.

Constantly struggling,
they live by their graveside,
barely surviving
the war zone of their souls;

with fading hope,
with feeble strength, and
with army of misfortunes.

The unfortunate warriors, fight relentlessly
with forces bearing torments,

until they are awarded
victory over calamity.

— ❧ —

Clear Mind

Luggage of past,
    turns pillars of strength
    into heaps of disappointments,
    making one incompetent
    to stand ground.

Broken spirits,
    dissipate confidence,
    decline efforts
    to pick up fallen strength.

Clear mind,
    restores self-assurance,
    provides drive to secure solid ground
    with unconstrained decisions.

— ✁ —

History Rests in...

History rests in comfort
    inside books,
    until scholars revise it
    time and again.

Civilization breathes underground
    until archeologists unearth it,
    with their spades of knowledge.

Victories and defeats resign
    in verses and stories,
    until writers and poets revise them
    with approval or condemnation.

Veterans and martyrs
    reside in our hearts and minds
    (permanently),
    with enduring approval,
    with eternal respect.

— ❧ —

Anger

Anger,
    fire burning by the house of straw,
    beast with a hidden paw,
    happiness in flames,
    bitterness unfolds its realm.

Anger,
    suffocating smoke,
    inferno in hell,
    destroys wits, spirits, and talents,
    converts comfortable situation
    into tumultuous condition.

Anger,
    injures tender hearts of family and friends,
    fatal for reliability,
    burden for relationships,
    dilemma for loved ones and associates,
    undignified for a civilized person.

— ✿ —

Looking Back

Looking back at life I realize,

Torments,
    threaten boundaries of sanity
    turning pulsating heart
    into a motionless stone, and
    rational mind into a senseless block.

Betrayals,
    cause anger, grief, and confusion,
    attract undeviating aggravation,
    keep (one) in intimidating pressure.

Anguish,
    helps wander off
    authentic path of accomplishments,
    disrupts life of purpose and reason.

Thorns of despair,
    rupture joyful thoughts,
    hopelessness makes to the heart.

Pain,
    provides constant sufferings,
    obliterates healthy body and collected mind.

Disappointment,
    causes distress and frustration,
    invites regret and discontent.

Appeased mind,
    maintains healthy outlook,
    positive attitude,
    strengthens shaky bonds.

Act of exoneration,
    liberates soul,
    leads to sensible grounds.

— ~ —

Facts of Life

Traveling from ignorance to knowledge I realized

"Actions and emotions dwell
in judgments,
fair conclusions materialize
in honest decisions,"
friendship and generosity survive
in kind hearts,
healthy seeds produce
healthy crops.

Swimming depth of sentiments I discovered

"An ounce of prudence engenders
a pound of intelligence,"
like a small dose of medicine generates
a lifetime of prevention
against perilous infection.

Exploring substance of life I uncovered

"Stress like a friend foretells us"
to restrain provoked emotions, or
cheerfulness and insight will vanish
in resentment,
like lifetime's treasured possession
in flames.

Crawling towards age of maturity I discovered

    Opportunities raze obstacles,
        success eliminates failures,
  creative minds venture diverse territories
        for broader prospects,
        for extensive wisdom,
 like archeologists break new grounds
        for exceptional disclosures.

After learning facts of life I acknowledged

    Common sense armors
       war of reasons
          against unfair events,
             like well-equipped army
                against ill prepared division.

— ❧ —

Two Faces of Silence

I

A feeling of contentment,
A cooling shade of comfort,
A sanctuary to obtain calm,
A salutary stroll to wonderland of mind,
A soothing visit to land of blessings,
A time to scale wall of reasons,
A chance to rearrange priorities,
A moment to take a hard look at life
A flight from misery to embrace tormented soul,
A refuge for sweet dreams,
A freedom to run free in imagination,
An artful exaggeration of serenity,
An opportunity to consummate happiness,
A pastoral tranquility achieved delightfully.

II

A quilt of gloom,
A siege for free existence,
Anxiety cold and scummy,
Air soaked with apprehension,
A self-imposed restriction on communication,
A distance attained pointlessly,
Aloneness experienced unnecessarily,
Anxiety acquired brainlessly,
Disappearance under the cloud of desperation,
A journey towards unhealthy emotions,
A stormy sail on waters of panic,
An edge that makes hurt feel heavenly,
A pain so great that dare not be felt,
A fine line between genius and insanity.

— ❧ —

Sense of Humor

Sense of humor,
    tranquil ease,
    consoling peace,
    symphony of relief,
    flow of breeze,
    compensation for insolence,
    medication for contempt,
    benevolence for malevolence.

Sense of humor,
    eternal summer, warm forever;
    priceless therapy for anxious moments,
    invaluable gift for wits and spirits,

presents hostile messages in light colors
    for jaded minds,
    for weary hearts.

"Dust your sense of humor
and keep it handy within your reach."

    Brightness and darkness
    amend face of our universe,

    integrity and sincerity
    vary from humiliation and arrogance,

    rudeness and politeness
    differ in properties,

    feline's purr
    resonates mightier than a growl.

To assign offense some softness,
to alter unpleasant approach,
to eliminate humiliation, and disgrace,
to keep balance between thorns and roses,
to confer life with reverence and respect,

"Dust your sense of humor
and keep it handy within your reach."

— ❧ —

Soldier be at Peace

Soldier be at Peace.
Miseries of war left behind
are nightmares of past.

Journey of life—
full of adventure, full of plight.
welcome pleasure, embrace life.

Haunted past,
devastated present,
uncertain future,

replace them with

overlooked past,
ambitious present, and
glorious future.

Wake up from gloomy night,
greet morning light,
visualize happiness,
savor delights of life.

Ambitions and perceptions,
warm heart,
enhance confidence,
curtail fears,
console restless soul.

Forget
    adversaries,
abandon
    bitterness,
desert
    fearfulness,

March diligently towards field of relaxation,
rejoice cheerful heart and tranquil state of mind.

— ॐ —

Words of Appreciation

Words of Appreciation
    Sing sweetest song to
    desperate souls
    who wander around for
    recognition and attention.

Words of Appreciation
    Immense therapy
    for uncertainty and frustration,
    significant satisfaction
    for anxious beings.

Words of Appreciation
    Enormous pleasure,
    appeases restless hearts,
    captures nomadic minds,
    equips life with dignity and composure.

— ❧ —

Marriage

Marriage like a profession,
demands full time attention.

Partners secure fence of mutual reliance
around fortress of reciprocal affection,
securing boundaries of varied identities.

Mutual respect and collaborated decisions—
the indispensable components
of successful married life,
nourish couple's relationship
with warmth, love, and attention

helping them stay side by side
with trusting heart and perpetual understanding
during inconsistencies of life.

Husband and wife,
guardian of each other's happiness,
reside in solemn joy
rejoicing shared understanding and
heartwarming reverence,
as heat in sun, as fragrance in gardens,
until Providence separates them eternally.

Old Age

*Saving fragile pride…mellowing
down with the sunset of life.*

Before Resting in Soft Peace

Retreating from fullness of her past,
sitting cradled in pensive thoughts,
accepting her slipping reign,
deprived of prized strength,
acknowledging nothing stays unchanged,
old age decided
not to deviate from elegance.

Saving fragile pride,
mellowing down with sunset of life:

deserting random actions,
    avoiding unseen tides,
        suppressing cherished notions—
            fantasy of omnipotence,
                old age bade farewell
                    to her majestic past.

Accommodating
    Substantial Loss,
Neglecting
    Apprehensive Heart,
Tolerating
    Alliance with Discontent
        like a mountaineer
            canceling ascent
                due to perilous conditions,

Old age strove
    to domicile
        with forbearance
            before resting in soft peace.

— ॐ —

A Dose of Bitter Medicine

Moving forward after prime of life,
    with commitment,
        endurance, and
            assertion,
like mothers exercise for their children,

I reconciled, adjusted, and advanced
to settle in unperturbed state
before sundown of my life.

Distancing from conventional burdens,
adopting flexible set of regulations,
    with mature perception,
    with optimum patience,

to save myself from strain of distress,
caused by partial autonomy
of making decisions for my feeble life.

I strove
    to terminate disappointments,
    eliminate frustrations,
    eradicate agitation,
I swallowed my pride
like a dose of bitter medicine.

— ❧ —

Rocking in Past Glories

When memories of past and present
begin to blend,
mode of life starts to change,
presence is less felt,
things get beyond hands.

Eccentric thoughts occupy my mind
when I see my ninety-year-old father
sitting in a recliner, involved in quiet.

Has he been thinking about himself:

"Life drags like a wounded snake,
and is felt only by aches and pains"
personal credits gone in vain;

I elegize life vigorously spent
by placing a wreath on energy and strength.

Empty of recent memories,
rocking in past glories,
dealing with a list of
do's and don'ts
shaking eminence and pride
off my ripened tree,

I sit calmly asserting serenity and grace
with abandoned fear of death,
waiting for eternal liberty.

— ❧ —

Short-lived Glory

During spring of our lives
we bloom like daffodils,
celebrating summer of our youth,

Before
    short-lived glory
    journeys towards
    autumn of our existence,

Stealing
    energy and spirits
    from days of our choice,
    leaving us
    with shallow wits and sharp anxieties.

Limitations
    appear slowly,

Uncertainties
    replace self-assurance,

Dependency
    displays its haggard face,

Self-reliance
    melts like wax under the sun,

Intelligence
    Threatens to step out of its residence,

Former accomplishments
    lose significance,

Fatigue
    administers days,

Sleep
    neglects nights,

until permanent winter of mortal life
lays us for eternal rest.

— ❧ —

Bereavement

Losing a loved one—
an irreplaceable loss,
causes immense grief and
feeling of deprivation.

Melancholic Heart and Solicitous Mind

Feelings of deprivation and longing
knocked me down
with excruciating grief
when news of your saying final goodbye
reached me
accompanied with
deepest sorrow and greatest loss.

I tried not to turn to stone and
tarnish my soul in bereavement.
Melancholy heart ached to mourn,
but solicitous mind desired
to celebrate the life well lived.

I struggled to search for peace
by turning intense sadness
inside out and console myself
by wrapping arms around
precious memories of my pastoral past:
when fragrance of
fatherly love kept me inebriated
with affection and benevolence,
I cherished your care and
attention while growing up.

Story time at night,
(spent with you),
was a magical pleasure;
the interesting tales and fables,
besides taking me
to wonderland of museums, parks, and zoo,
introduced me to life of purpose and aspiration.

Your treasured presence in my school,
while I played basketball and
participated in stage plays,
was a source of immense pleasure.

Father, you engraved values of
honesty and chastity in my young heart,
you diligently tried to infuse
knowledge and common sense in me, and
your wisdom implanted seeds of awareness
in my inexperienced mind.

I could always turn to you for advice.
After every crisis of my life,
you stood firm by my side
to reassemble my strength, and
to protect me from falling apart.

Your intense interest in reading and
choice of moving forward with time,
benefited me and my children, and would
influence my generations to come.

Father, I witnessed you going through
good times and bad, with dignity and grace.
Your relentless efforts and admirable talents,
with unwavering resolve and resilience,
helped you overcome turbulent times successfully.

You shared your good fortune
with less fortunate ones
with transcendent wisdom and
extraordinary generosity.

Father, I applaud the life you lived;
people like you are not born every day.

The valuable lessons learned from your life,
would help me live by your golden rules.
The echo of your august love
would always assist me through tough times.

I am so very much proud of being
Your daughter.
Thank you very much, father
for molding me into the person I am.

— ❧ —

A Faint Smile

I had never seen smile wear off my mother's face.
    It welcomed anxious hearts,
    embraced neglected souls,
like sun would warm someone in bitter cold.

Mother was accessible for abandoned ones
    with generosity of compassion,
    with abundance of benevolence,
    with kindness and consideration.

Her shinning eyes captivated hearts of forsaken ones.

Nature was enough to incite smile on mother's face.
    She defied complexities of life bravely,
    by confronting them courageously,

believing

if problems are endured with valiant smiling face,
    joviality beats malignity,
    exuberance confronts sufferings,
    cheerfulness honors life.

During prime of her life,
calamity raided mother's energetic body,
like enemy would attack a foreign territory.

Infection assaulted spine,
depriving her of walking ability.

Mother slipped into deep coma,
illustrious smile abandoned her once radiant face.

Barely attached to the universe,
unaware of surroundings,
empty of happy memories,
graceful in seventy year old slender body,
with perfect comfort of her inside,

mother lay in bereavement bed, motionless,
black and gray hair encircled beautiful oval face,
closed soft brown eyes,
void of cheerful dreams,
saddened family and friends.

Frail expressionless existence,
without radiant smile,
pierced loved ones' hearts,
bringing them to near-anesthetized state.

Ten days and ten nights went by
since beautiful legendary smile,
deserted mother's once lively face,
before a tender touch of
my father's hand on her forehead,
brought her awake.

Facial muscles struggled to bring old smile back;

a moment later,
      with a faint smile on her feeble face,
      mother closed her tender eyes to infinity
      leaving jewel of her precious memory
      in family's forlorn hearts.

— ઌ —

A Goodbye that was Never Said

On the floor of intensive care,
where sorrows crawled
like shadows on wall,
where life and death dwelt together
with shades—white and pale,

where my agonized soul
searched for solace,
where melancholy smiles,
on your sad face, confirmed:

> *I have done my share,*
> *and shall leave the rest in Almighty's care.*

Thank you my friend, for being my strength
during the time of distress and fear.

> Ben Sabbatino
> (now a departed soul), and I
> worked together on hospital floor,
> sharing losses and calamities of strangers,
> before vicious monster
> attacked my friend's energetic existence.

Ben left hospital determined
to be back victorious,
but mournful moments had different motives.

News of your demise, my friend, tore me asunder.

I wished to be at your side
to attire anguish with hope and promise,
while you struggled for life,
before closing your eyes forever.

Dear Ben,
I wasn't ready, to see sufferings
on your ever-smiling face, and
witness the vessel of joy,
with cargo of tranquility,
vanish in the ocean of infinity.

I wasn't prepared, my friend,
to let go the harvest of our friendship—
solace, support, and understanding.

The treasure was mine to keep safe for life.

Beloved friend,
you still are alive in my heart and mind.

When mortality visits a helpless patient,
and misery unveils itself on his agonized face,
and my presence makes no difference,
in his existence, or in his final moments,

I still hear your reassuring voice:

You have done your share,
and should leave the rest in Almighty's care.

It confirms your presence,
it collects my anxious existence
to prevent me from losing my strength
to remorseful feeling of regret.

— ॐ —

Infant Joys, Matured Sorrows

I still wore little pink shoes, and
played with children in the neighborhood,
when mom walked me to your door.

    I waited nervously
    in living room, before
    noticing you on a wheelchair
    moving towards me
    wearing a frail smile on your pale face.

A little girl of my age
looked at me with eagerness and inquired:

    Would you be my friend?

    With great excitement,
    without a speck of doubt,
    with truthfulness of my heart,
    I nodded in affirmation.

Your welled-up eyes sparkled in elation.

You, my friend,
    a fountain of love,
    a model of pleasantness,
    a portrayal of audacity,
    a monument of trust, and
    an example of incredible valor,
were confined inside your house,
with fragile existence,
with infant joys, and
with matured sorrows.

Leukemia had raided
every core of your being
like malaria would
soil a fragile body with
chills, fever, and sweat…

Time spent together was my pleasure,
before you rested motionless,
     with deteriorating state,
     with failing breath,
     with deadliest smile
on your bluish face.

Spending few days in a quiet state,
closing once radiant eyes
     with hidden fears,
     with give-in spirits,

You slept in Holy silence
to be awoken no more.

— ॐ —

In Memory of Dr. Emil Orsini

Your life,
    full of purpose, full of passion,
        your prominent place—
            hearts and minds of your
                family, friends, and colleagues.

Beneficiaries of your skills:
    patients of North York General Hospital.
        Your proficiency, your contemplation—
            patient's treasured possessions.

Your skilled hands on diseased joints,
    their precious gift
        for pain-free existence after
            agonizing orthopedic invasions.

Your sense of humor,
    your encouraging smiles—
        their insurance for successful recuperation
            from extremely painful joint surgeries.

We, the patients,
    heard knell of your parting day
        with bemoaning hearts,
            realizing the colossal loss of our captain
                who helped us win intricate battles
                against painful, unhealthy joints.

Dear Dr. Orsini,
    Your eternal absence from our lives
        caused a silent scream
            from the core of our existence and
                grieved us permanently.

Your immortal memory,
    embossed on dismal hearts,
        besides being an extremely dedicated
            and enormously gifted surgeon,

you were an affectionate human being
of multiple capabilities and varied talents.

— ❧ —

Nine-Eleven

Our foundation was renewed with steel, cement, and concrete, saturated with blood of our loved ones.

Our Great Nation Stood Tall

Angry but warm, furious but strong,
our nation fathomed its grief with stormy calm.
A religion, twisted and used,
to turn our home front into front line
to justify a cemetery in our midst!

Fear extended its domain on September the 11th, 2001:
Twin Towers brought down to their remains.

The tragedy cut deep into our soul,
thousands of occupants vanished
in the flowing river of ash.

A mourning nation shed tears of anguish
for thousands of their innocents.

Fire trucks engulfed in fire,
hundreds of firefighters
buried alive under crumbling towers,
ambulances turned upside down,
sirens shricking, lights revolving,
scattered debris, papers and pieces of glass,
along with human body parts,
introduced the horrifically changed diagram of
the financial district of New York.

Thousands of faces daubed in dust and blood,
a daunting mob of human beings,
anxious, screaming, and howling,
struggled to get away from horrific death.

Dark clouds of smoke, like thick midnight fog,
cloaked twisted metal exposed from the towers.
Disaster shook us to the core of our existence.

Our nation was assaulted, but not morally diminished.

> To support the nation in her darkest moment,
> to recover cold bodies from fluid inferno of ground zero,
> to save loved ones from mouth of hell,
> to negotiate fears,
> to demonstrate strength,
> to reconstruct our memories of ones travelled to heaven,

grieving nation joined hands to confront the colossal challenge.

> The bravest of our country
> toiled, unfailingly, round the clock
> for those erased savagely
> from the face of their beloved land.

Our great nation stood tall to face chaos and destruction.

> Fury focused on our adversaries,
> targeting a part of enemy's territory,
> our nation looked for justice, not for revenge.

Our nation was ready to confront the enormous challenge.

To differentiate between love and hate,
to save innocents from hunger, disease, and bitter cold,
living in enemy's territory,
our benevolent nation delivered
food, medicines, and clothes to the needy.
Our nation proved its love for humanity,
leaving punishment for the devil in Almighty's hand.

Sad moments, sober times,
hopes lost, promises made,
recognition of those
crowned with eternal liberty.

Deceased firefighters and servicemen,
for their sacrifices and dedication,
were recognized posthumously;
tributes were paid to deceased citizens and foreigners, alike.

Enemies, neglecting the golden rule of co-existence,
overlooked multi-cultural, multi-colored face of their religion,
ignorantly believed to secure a place in heaven
after inflicting us with irreplaceable loss
and unimaginable sufferings.

They miserably failed to sever the soul of our nation,
and were left frightened with assorted fear of death and penance,
with their days numbered, with their fate pronounced.

How much of us got lost,
how much of us was gathered?

Though our patience and tolerance
were stretched to their lengths,
our foundation was renewed
with steel, cement, and concrete,
saturated with blood of our loved ones.

Our nation stood united like a solid column of cement.

Enemies witnessed beauty
come out of their ugly deeds:

we nurtured our dignity,
we strengthened our courage

to manage the catastrophe
of unimaginable magnitude.

Our great nation stood tall to face the chaos and destruction.

— ҩ —

Soy Milk and Chocolate Cookie

Would you like to try some soy milk
and a piece of chocolate cookie?
They're fresh and tasty.
Promoting her products in the supermarket,
said the green-eyed, blonde lady.

Let's see what you promote.
I said,
trying to gulp mouthful of soy milk,
and reaching out for a piece of chocolate cookie.

I have a few questions to ask,
the lady interrupted
before I swallowed soy milk and chocolate cookie;

Where are you from?
She inquired.

Without giving me a chance to respond,
the green-eyed lady resumed her talk:

My daughter is dating an architect from Pakistan,
she will marry the gentleman to follow her heart.
How long the marriage would last?
was the question she asked.

With curiosity and concern combined,
she looked at me with inquisitive eyes.

What can I say, Ma'am?
Marriage is a gamble,
Let's keep our fingers crossed
and hope for the best.
I replied.

People in Pakistan do not like Americans,
Muslims hate Christians.
Pakistanis are terrorists like Afghanis.
Won't my daughter's safety be my concern,
if she decides to live in a terrorist country!
The lady spoke all her fears aloud,
her illusive thoughts left me bewildered.
A wave of grief passed through my existence
generating a funereal silence in my heart.

Seeing fear and distrust in her eyes,
remembering the brutality of Nine-Eleven,
I was caught between her ignorance and concerns.

Talk about Pakistan brought back the memories
I thought I was over and done with.

I understand your anxiety Ma'am,
but I am not sure how to answer your questions!
I said to the lady while tasting chocolate cookie:

Pakistanis and Afghanis
are freedom-loving sweet people,
not too different from Americans;
terrorists are individuals, not a Nation, or a Religion.
I concluded the conversation.

With sour flavor in my mouth,
without remembering the taste of
chocolate cookie or soy milk,
visualizing the barbarity of September the 11th,
condemning heartless barbarians, and
not comprehending hatred against innocents,
I left the supermarket with sorrowful heart.

Does it make a difference
if someone is
a Muslim, a Jew, a Hindu,
a Sikh, a Buddhist or a Christian!

Brotherhood, love and harmony—
the components of every faith,
shelter innocents against violence
irrespective of their color, race, and religion.

Swimming in the stream of consciousness,
I came back home from the grocery store
carrying a basket full of anxieties, dreads, and sorrows.

— ҩ —

Curiosity and others

Certain observations, events, emotions, and memories invite creative minds to express life elaborately.

Life Long Commitment

As Sofia stormed out of the shopping mall,
a knot of anxiety formed in Steve's stomach;
his magnificent world of love,
melted in slush of embarrassment.

Hours later in their bed,
lying beside himself,
embraced by magnanimous
shame, despair, and run-out fate,
sequence of events
spiked Steve's apprehensive mind.

He journeyed through a procession of thoughts:

You're the queen of my heart,
my first love and the last.

A beautiful girl of twenty-two,
a tulip in bloom,
with seductive face and captivating smile,
had fulfilled my existence
as a treasured partner of my life.

Sofia's obsession
for gourmet food and entertainment,
befriended a lady next door—
a sociable person, an exceptional cook,
a single parent to her six year old,

ready to share recipes,
quick to organize picnics and parties.

Time spent among the four
multiplied fun in their lives.

Sofia and Steve were among the few
enjoying blissful harmonious relationship:

calamities ignored the couple,
jewel of mutual trust and reliability
crowned their married life,

until Steve made a phone call to his wife:

Due to prolonged engagement at office,
unfortunately, our anniversary dinner
will be delayed by an hour.

Sofia decided to venture out before
her beloved husband arrived.
Strolling in a nearby shopping mall,
as she negotiated a corner,
a shocking sight appalled her;
burst of anger shattered her trusting heart,
dragon of infidelity poisoned her happy habitat.

Engrossed in each other,
walked hand in hand,
Steve and the mother of six year old.

Inferno of resentment
ignited Sofia from crown to sole,
dressing her in the robe of smoldering anger.

Steve's betrayal left her with
obliterated map of their married life.

Essence of cordial relationship,
evaporated like fragrance
from weathered flowers,
leaving blooming partnership
under sweltering heat,

passion and warmth became
improbable and hypocritical substances
of their callously susceptible union.

Sleepless and anxious in his bed, Steve realized,
his betrayal had created an icy indifference
between him and his beloved wife,
turning their bed of love, pleasure, and comfort
into bed of (his) guilt, disgrace, and regret.

— ৵ —

A Talent

"Fault finding is a talent
ignorant love to have.

They keep it sharpened
by using 20-20 vision."

Those who judge, of course, are the smartest ones.

    Mistakes alienate them,
    wisdom embraces them with open arms,
    and keeps them on the right path:

guiding their attitude,
for the self-assigned task,
to encourage continuity
of special obligation,
    with diligence
    with intelligence.

Ignorant cannot be proven wrong
    as they are the wisest ones.

— ❧ —

Curiosity

Lost in labyrinth of life,
determined to leave path of ignorance behind,
curious to follow road
leading to truth and authenticity,

    I explored possibilities
    to grow inside,
    and live a dynamic life.

    I endeavored to invade
    realm of reason and knowledge,
    seeking intellectual minds with eagerness.

Curiosity led me towards awareness,
coaching my ignorant self
to brew wine of life
with vision and motivation
by expanding horizon of my mind.

Ailing Emotions

A planeload full of Wounded Emotions,
took off from the runway of Battered Sentiments;

> bumpy ride, caused by
> Sweltering Winds of Frustrations,
> brought down the fateful plane,
> in the Field of Disappointments,
> before reaching its destination—
> the State of Perception.

> Ambulances equipped with
> Slanders of Awareness and Recognition,
> were dispatched to the site of devastation,
> brought victims to triage for assessment,
> to Hospital of Ailing Emotions.

Some suffered serious injuries,
others endured minor cuts and bruises,
few bled profusely, and
needed instantaneous care.

Self-esteem and Validity,
> were resuscitated on the spot,
> for fatal conditions.

Honor and Integrity,
> though wounded severely,
> survived with profound scars.

Happiness and Joviality,
> casualties beyond recognition,
> ended up in hospital's morgue.

Reliability and Emotional Help
    arrived on the scene of devastation
    to sustain safety assurance.

Investigators from the
Hospital of Ailing Emotions,
reached this conclusion:

    Airport authorities of Battered Sentiments
    should have grounded the ill-fated flight
    of Wounded Emotions
    until pilot had recovered
    from Traumatic Cerebral Upheaval.

— ❦ —

Enormous Piece of Cloud

I'm an enormous piece of cloud,
moving over the universe,
like a gypsy on earth,
or wandering imagination of a poet.

I float above mountains, oceans, and prairies,
presenting phantom of darkness;

my mammoth circumference
    blocks sunlight,
sheets of rain
    turn day into night.

I permit thunder to rumble,
and deliver wine of life,
by rolling white pearls,
    to drought-stricken crops
    to enrich land for harvest.

Green fields are my emerald gift
for hardworking farmers
to spare them from hunger.

My presence makes a day
dim and grim.
After dark murky clouds
finish their assignment,
I advise the sun to shower golden rays
to wash face of the earth.

I travel uninterrupted above the universe,
with multiple rationales:

my overly generous supply of moisture,
causes havoc to habitats,
destroying precious human lives,
and possessions of their lifetime.

But I also
nourish land with sufficient moisture
to save it from a looming drought,
and direct showers to deserts
to save lives of bone-tired thirsty travelers.

— ❧ —

Excel and Rely

Excel in diligence,
Rely on your heart.

Recreate the diagram of your life,
    consider your intellect for assistance
        to modify manuscript of your actions,
            like an intellectual scholar confident of his potentials.

Be prepared to negotiate ups and downs of your life
    with patience and perseverance.

Challenge your worth
    to new heights,
        restore confidence
            after every plight.

Excel in diligence,
Rely on your heart.

— ❧ —

Seasons

Dressed in tender green,
trees standing by the side of streets,
flourish from spring to summer,
for lovers to yield pleasure,
before season's numerous objectives,
deprive them of emeralds.

Multicolored apparel—
temptation for streets
like assorted jewels,
attraction for ladies.

Strong winds,
envious of colorful leaves,
bring rainbow on streets.

Stretched-out arms of trees,
wrapped in thick white sheets,
enchant streets
as the first snowfall of the season
mesmerizes small children.

Standing by the side of streets,
waiting to be fully clad in green,
trees attired in frozen outfit
from head to feet,
decide to hibernate,
until winter retreats.

— ❧ —

On Cloud Nine

Alliance in jubilation,
affection in bloom,
smiles in abundance,
pleasure approved by the season.

Engulfed in gold,
warmed with passion,
lovers sang in elation
(not necessarily in attendance).

Under glory's wings,
embracing cloud nine,
together they flew towards paradise
abandoning their doubts in thin air.

Collaborated with destiny,
cuddled in authenticity, they
unclothed their hidden thoughts,
dwelling in absolute passion.

— ও —

In Sapphire Blue

Commitment
   in vigilance,

compassion
   in elegance,

professionalism
   in grace,

diligent ladies and gentlemen
   in sapphire blue,
on the meticulous floors of
   North York General Hospital,

are proficiently organized

to help,
to prepare,
to collaborate, and
to perform assigned duties,

with enhanced confidence,
with superb spirits,

holding hearts
   of patients and families
in gentle smiles
   on their benevolent faces.

— ৯ —

Words Are Our Friends

"Words stand powerless in dictionary
waiting to be used"
with depth, beauty, and energy.

Utilize them in expressions
with elegance and deliberation,
knit them accurately
into tapestry of life.

    Bare your pleasures,
    Mirror your pain,

    Defuse your thoughts,
    Enhance your intelligence,

    Rescue your memory
    from unnecessary confinement.

Dig deep into reservoirs
of your recollection,

    surface radiant ideas,
    interesting stories, and
    deeply buried emotions.

Consider your dreams gracious friends,
treasure your ambitions like bars of gold,
write them in inebriating inscriptions,

    for constant reminder,
    for lasting enjoyment.

Let imagination run far and wide
allowing it to entwine with
happiness and promise;
convert it in warm verses, and passionate manuscripts,
melt them on sheets like ice in hot sun.

Cord of memory carries experiences
good and bad, happy and sad,

    Compose them, argue them,
    for and against.

    Analyze them, apply them,
    experiment them,

    Transfer them in black and white
    with humor and grace.

"Words are friends visited by us again and again,"

    to negotiate our experiences,
    to discuss our judgments,

    to converse problems
    to state their solutions
    acquired from lifetime of evidence,

    pleasant, atrocious, and catastrophic,
    friendly, jovial and tragic,
    enigmatic, appalling and dynamic.

Empower your scripts
to mesmerize readers,

Emit love
	to extend benevolence,
	to eradicate hostility,
	to discourage estrangement.

Enhance compassion
with intellect and perception.

Organizing words
with colossal diligence and perfect precision.

"Words are friends visited by us again and again."

— ॐ —

Colossal Glory

On Justine's birth in November 2010
my friend Robin was conferred
Colossal Glory
along with little angel's
delighted young parents.

Granddaughter's heart-warming
company
rocks grandma's soul
in divine felicity.

Robin's cathedral of love
(for her treasured grandchild)
is on green island of pleasure.

Flowers of
affection and jubilation,
grow around grandma's
lush green shrine of care.

Fountains of happiness
shower
pearls of blessings, and
those are all theirs.

May grandma and granddaughter
enjoy cathedral of love forever.

(A present for my dearest friend Robin Newell
on her 60th Birthday)

— ॐ —

T-Chamber vs. T-Chamber

Invitation,
(kind of mandatory for T-Chamber),
arrives every four to five months
from Dentistry on Danforth.

It's an immaculate venue
arrayed with some of
the most skillful and courteous people
city should be proud of.

Politeness
enriches their smiling faces,
skills
ornament their gentle hands,
clients' satisfaction
is their commitment.

The place is equipped
with meticulous gadgets
to preserve invitees' oral health.

Clients enter the venue
a bit anxious, a bit embarrassed, but
leave the site at ease
with enormously sparkling teeth,
with thoroughly clean mouths.

After hygienist's scrupulous accomplishment,
soft-spoken proficient doctor,
accompanied by experienced vigilant eyes,
(that never miss a problem in mouth),
examines T-Chamber for crisis.

Invasive procedures (if needed)
are performed
(of course with clients' permission),
with minimum possible torment.

T-Chamber is extremely susceptible to negligence:

poor oral hygiene causes havoc
turning Teeth Chamber into Torture Chamber.

Mathematical Death

I lay content in bed.
I close my eyes.
I see some fog
and hear a voice:

"Your life, like a cloud, must part."

    "I feel flying back and forth in space.
    I watch helplessly my failing breaths,"
    I see shining light above me and realize:
    life will say goodbye before its time.

I begin to assess my own state:

months of insomnia,
lack of movement,
abundance of unhealthy food,
affluence of caffeine,
frequent use of alcohol, and
regular doses of marijuana.

    It can't be true,
    I shout in disbelief and
    "open my eyes into the rising sun,
    and take a sigh of relief to be alive."

I open a window,
savor breaths of fresh air,
wipe beads of perspiration from forehead.

I sit in a recliner embracing life,
and assess my fairly healthy routine:

except for few fraudulent habits,
I've avoided pernicious lifestyle.

I wonder
if I already have invited my end
or nature will take its course!

*(Lines in quotation were given in class
to write a poem around them.)*

From Harsh Winter to Pleasant Spring

When cold winds try to take advantage of naked trees,
and glassy popsicles provide them with clothing,
trees stand shivering,
waiting to be attired in tender green.

The spectacle of trees
motivates spectators to make prophecies:

>Some say severe winter may stay longer
>like a highly skilled player on a baseball field.

>Some say winter may change abruptly,
>like decision of an immature adult.

>Others think winter may descend gradually,
>like old age on a lively young lady.

I have calculated probabilities:

>winter may attract
>large amounts of snow and ice,
>it may break previous records of extremes
>by ascending to its ever highest peak
>like a seasoned athlete touches his
>career's utmost limits.

Or, winter may linger mildly
>with flurries and sleet,
>with intoxicating breeze,
>with frequent gold beams,
>with cloudy ecstasies, and

it may convince spring to entertain us early
after adversities of bitter freeze.

I am prepared to accommodate
the diverse company, and provide comfort
to dissimilar guests, with appropriate requisites:

    shawls, hats, scarves, gloves, and heavy coats
        to welcome severe winter, and
            much needed warmth against relentless cold;

        light sweaters, capes, hot beverages and cozy rooms
           to greet lingering mild cold, and to dream
              for early appearance of blooming spring.

— ❧ —

My Shrine

To say my prayers,
I built a shrine not far from me
to thank, to praise, and to ask for forgiveness

for sins I commit—
unconsciously, and sometimes
due to my sheer ignorance.

When unspoken grief tightens its grip on me,
solemnly I pray and request the Almighty
to bless me with peace and endurance,
and enable me to find an appropriate solution.

I do not have to walk
to a designated place,
wait for a particular day,
save a definite time,
use a specific language,
or follow a certain practice,
to be with my gracious God.

He lives in the temple,
built in my heart,
with His Majestic Grace
above and beyond all our
self-imposed rules and restrictions.

— ॐ —